MYRAA KAUR

Sophie and Rory's Adventures

Summer Camp Mystery

BookLeaf
Publishing
www.bookleafpub.com

Dedication

To my family for helping me throughout
my writing journey

CHAPTER 1

The Weather

"I have a great feeling about today!" I said.

For once, it was not raining. The sun shone brightly as students chattered.

My name is Sophie Collins. I absolutely adore reading, and I have a passion for fashion. People say I have a very curious mind. Rory Anorra is my best friend. She has luscious red hair that are usually braided. Rory has a lisp, but I still love the way she sounds.

I will be her friend forever and ever.

Students started to quiet down while our teachers explained our itinerary for the day.

We didn't pay close attention to who was in our first summer camp activity except for the part where our names got called. Rory squealed with excitement as we found out we were in the same group.

Our first activity was a forest walk.

"Boring," I groaned.

The group set off for our activity, and we followed them.

CHAPTER 2

The Cabin

We walked for what felt like hours and saw many things: ants, butterflies, birds, various types of plants.

But soon, Rory and I started slowing down.
Before we realised, we had lost the whole
group! Stuck in the forest with nobody in sight,
I panicked. Suddenly, Rory spotted a tiny cabin.
We went to it only to see the door wide open.

"Please, can we go inside?" Rory pleaded.

It took me a while to say yes, I eventually gave in. We peeked in from behind the door. It was very dark inside. Rory reluctantly stepped in. I followed right behind. The door slammed shut right behind us because of the wind. I tried unlocking it, but it wouldn't budge. Rory already looked scared, so I didn't tell her. A window high out of reach was open, the floor creaked, the rooms looked old and broken. It was definitely abandoned. I knew I had to tell Rory the door wouldn't open, so I built up the courage, took one deep breath and got ready for the screaming.

"Rory, I have to tell you that the door is locked, it isn't opening," I explained.

I braced myself for the screaming, but nothing came out of her mouth other than a faint whimper. Her eyes were wide open when her jaw dropped.

The Attic

"How will we get out now?" Rory asked.

"I don't know," I muttered.

On a wooden table sat a radio, a cold cup of tea and a book whose pages were rapidly flapping from the wind. The pages were turning until it landed on one.

and climb through the vent,

It read: "Mary, use the ladder and climb through the vent" I wondered what it meant. I looked around and spotted a small, metal door that was closed. Rory was already banging on the door for help. I joined her on the windows. Nobody heard us. They were all gone, deep into the forest. We thought all hope was lost when the attic door flung wide open. Maybe it was just from the wind?

"Should we go in?" Rory asked.

I thought for a moment.

"I think we should," I replied, "it might be our only chance!"

We slowly approached the door and saw a deep, dark room above. Holding the railing, we stepped up the staircase. There was not a peep of light coming from the attic.

Boxes, light bulbs, ripped paper, carpets and much more filled the room, leaving no space to walk. We were in the room for so long that our eyes adjusted to the darkness so we could see what was around us. Scanning the room for the ladder, Rory saw steps with a red top. It was the ladder! Heaving it with all our might, we stumbled out to the lounge room while dropping it on the dirty brown floor.

CHAPTER 4

The Way Out

Our arms were tired after picking up the hefty ladder. It was worth it, though. At least now we had a way out. I still don't know how the pages landed on the one we needed and how the door opened by itself. The shivers came; it was like spiders were creeping all over me. We sat ourselves down on a torn couch. It had grey spots.

"Finally," Rory said, "how did the book do that?"

I rubbed my eyes while dusting myself off.

"I'm not sure," I answered. "Maybe it was just a coincidence."

With half of our energy back, we stood up from the couch. Rory was brave enough to climb the ladder to reach the vent door.

It flew open like birds' wings when they were about to take off for a long journey. Rory was already in the vent, and I looked at her with fear in my eyes.

"Come on, Sophie, you can do this," I thought to myself.

After a long, scary five steps, I was in the vent, crawling with Rory.

We jumped down onto the grass. I somehow went down with no fear. We slowly managed to find our way back to our assembly point.

CHAPTER 5

The Furious Instructor

Running through the bushes while twigs scratched us everywhere, we saw everybody sitting in the assembly area. A mosquito flashed before my eyes. It landed on my arm, trying to suck the blood out of me. I slapped it and moaned in pain. Our camp instructor stormed towards us with a big frown on her face.

"Where did you girls run off to?" she furiously asked.

"We lost the group in the middle of the forest," I explained.

"Well then, next time, you are going to walk right next to the instructors," she replied with her voice calming down.

Silently, we sat in an empty spot, listening to every word the teachers said, unlike last time. A boy a couple of rows in front of us fell on his back. We laughed out so loudly that everybody looked at us.

In our assigned sleeping cabins, Rory and I slept like babies after an exhausting day of mysteries and adventures. I wondered if we would have another day like this tomorrow.